ANIMAL ARTS AND CRAFTS

AFRICAN
ANIMAL CRAFTS

Annalees Lim

Gareth Stevens
PUBLISHING

CONTENTS

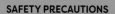

SAFETY PRECAUTIONS

We recommend adult supervision at all times while doing the activities in this book. Always be aware that craft materials may contain allergens, so check the packaging for allergens if there is a risk of an allergic reaction. Anyone with a known allergy must avoid these.

- Wear an apron and cover surfaces.
- Tie back long hair.
- Ask an adult for help with cutting.
- Check materials for allergens.

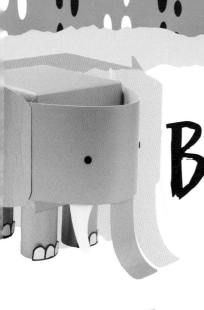

BEFORE YOU BEGIN

Africa is the second-largest continent on Earth. It is home to a huge variety of animals. Some of them have inspired the projects in this book. Which one will you choose to make first? You can find out lots of fun facts about the animals along the way.

Some of the equipment or materials needed to make these arts and crafts can be dangerous if they are not handled correctly. Please follow the instructions carefully and ask an adult to help you.

Some of the projects use paint and craft glue. When using these, always cover surfaces with layers of newspaper. Whenever you can, leave the project to dry before moving on to the next step. This avoids things getting stuck to each other or the paint getting smudged.

So, do you have your art and craft materials at the ready? Then get set to make some African animal arts and crafts.

STRIPY ZEBRA

Zebras are covered in black and white stripes. Each zebra has a stripy pattern that is one of a kind. You can make your zebra's pattern unique too!

YOU WILL NEED:

- Double-sided tape
- Googly eyes
- Scissors
- White and black felt
- White card stock (optional)
- Ruler
- Craft glue
- An adult to help you

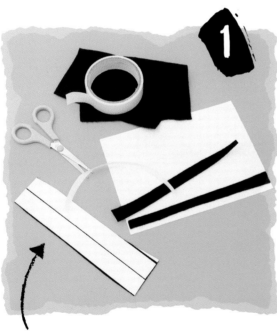

Ask an adult to help you cut a piece of white felt, 6 x 8 inches (15 x 20 cm), and a piece of black felt the same size. Stick three long strips of double-sided tape to the black felt. Now cut six sticky-backed strips of black felt and stick them onto the white felt to make stripes.

Roll your striped felt into a tube and stick the edges together using double-sided tape. If your felt is not thick enough to hold its shape, stick it to some white card stock first.

Cut out all the felt pieces as shown to make the head and legs.

Glue the felt pieces together to complete the head and legs. Stick them to the zebra body using double-sided tape.

Use double-sided tape to stick googly eyes to your zebra's face.

DID YOU KNOW?

Zebras don't lie down to sleep. They snooze while they are standing.

ZEBRA FACTS!

Zebras live together in herds on the African savanna. Every year, thousands of zebras migrate across the savanna, looking for fresh grasses and water.

A baby zebra is called a foal. It can run soon after it is born. This is important as zebras need to escape from predators, such as lions.

GIRAFFE FACTS!

Giraffes live on the African savanna. They hardly sleep, spending most of the day and night searching for food.

A giraffe's long neck helps it reach leaves in the treetops. Its long tongue helps it sort out the leaves from the thorns in its favorite food tree, the acacia.

GIRAFFE PUPPET

No two giraffes look exactly the same as they all have different markings. Have fun creating this giraffe puppet!

YOU WILL NEED:

- Five toilet paper rolls
- Yellow and brown paper
- Googly eyes
- Glue stick
- String
- Stapler
- 12-inch (30 cm) wooden dowel
- Scissors
- Ruler
- Tape
- An adult to help you

Ask an adult to help you cut three of the toilet paper rolls in half. Glue yellow paper to all the tubes. Put one short yellow tube aside. Cut out shapes from brown paper and glue them onto the remaining yellow tubes.

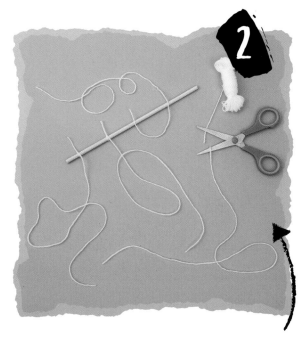

Cut four lengths of string, 12 inches (30 cm) long. Tie the string onto the wooden dowel. Thread the first string through the short yellow tube and use the stapler to staple it to the string, close to the wooden rod.

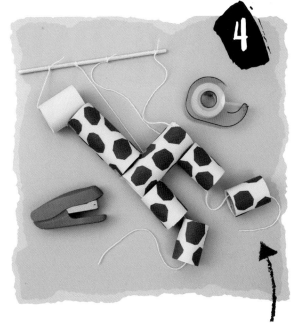

Thread two long patterned tubes onto the same string, stapling them in place. Tie the ends of the first and last strings together.

Thread two short tubes onto the end of one of the middle strings to form a leg. Staple them in place. Repeat for the other leg. Use tape to attach these strings to the body.

Cut into the head to make a mouth and cut some ears and a tail out of yellow card stock. Use strips of brown paper to make the mane, the tail end, and the hooves. Glue on the eyes.

DID YOU KNOW?

Giraffes are the tallest animals on Earth. A male giraffe can grow to about 18 feet (5.5 m) tall.

TISSUE PAPER LION

You can tell a male lion from a female by its large mane. Make a lion with a magnificent mane using lots of tissue paper.

YOU WILL NEED:

- Two brown, card-sized envelopes
- Orange tissue paper
- Glue stick
- Googly eyes
- Black felt-tip pen
- Scissors
- Tape
- An adult to help you

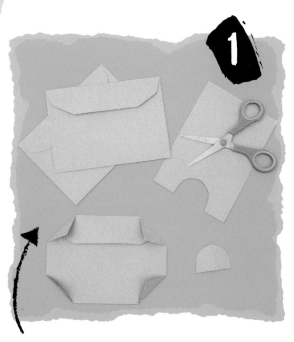

Fold in the corners of one of the envelopes. Take the other envelope and cut a small semicircle out of one of the short sides.

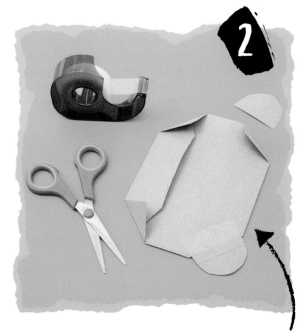

Open up the semicircle of paper and cut along the fold. Stick the semicircles onto two of the folded corners to finish the ears.

3

Cut rectangles of tissue paper. Fold them like a handheld fan and stick them to the back of the head. Spread them out

4

Add details to the face using the black felt-tip pen.

5

Glue the envelopes together to form the head and body of your lion. Glue on googly eyes.

DID YOU KNOW?

A male lion's mane grows longer and darker in color as he ages.

LION FACTS!

Wild lions used to live across Africa. Now most of them live in eastern and southern Africa.

Lions hunt grazing animals such as zebras, gazelles, and wildebeest.

Lions live in family groups called prides. Lionesses in the pride bring up their cubs together.

ELEPHANT FACTS!

Elephants live in family groups. The herd is usually made up of a grandmother, her sisters, their daughters, and the daughters' calves. The grandmother leads the herd.

Elephants have brains three times bigger than ours and are extremely clever. They can solve problems, have great memories, and show feelings for each other.

TISSUE BOX ELEPHANT

YOU WILL NEED:

- Gray paper
- Gray card stock
- Glue stick
- Scissors
- Tape
- Thin black marker
- Pencil
- White paper
- Two toilet paper rolls
- An adult to help you

African elephants are the largest land animals, weighing more than 13,000 pounds (5,900 kg). They eat lots of grass, roots, fruit, and bark every day.

Ask an adult to help you with the cutting in this project. Wrap the tissue box in gray paper, using tape to stick it down.

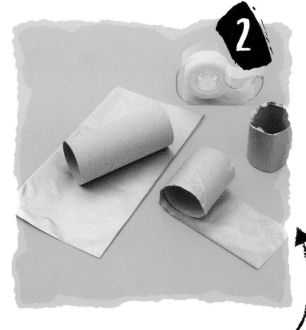

Cut the tubes in half and cover them in gray paper. Attach all the tubes to the bottom of the box using tape.

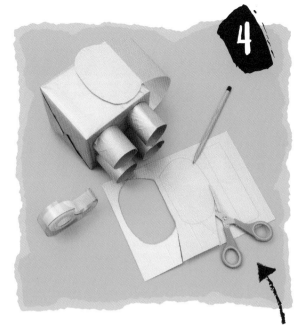

Cut out a rectangle of gray card stock and curve it around the front of the box to make the head. Attach it to the box with tape.

Cut out some ears, a trunk, and a tail from gray card stock. Stick all of them to your elephant.

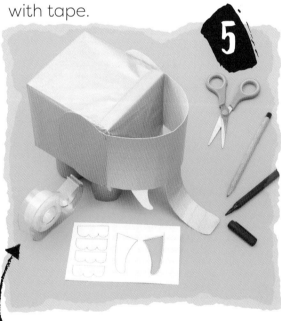

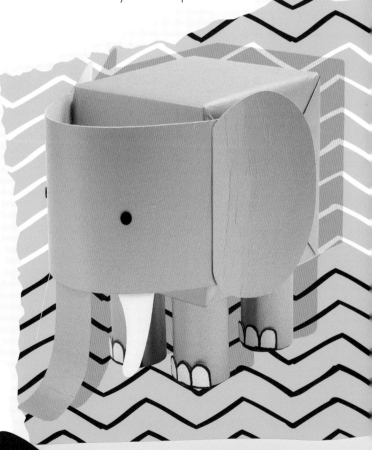

Draw two tusks and four sets of toes onto white paper. Cut them out and stick them to your elephant. Draw on eyes with the marker.

DID YOU KNOW?

Elephants are good swimmers. In deep water they use their trunks like a snorkel so that they can breathe.

DRINKING STRAW FLAMINGO

Flamingos are large pink birds that often stand on one leg. Have fun making your pink drinking straw flamingo!

YOU WILL NEED:

- Pink bendy drinking straws
- Pink tissue paper
- Pink, black, and orange paper
- Scissors
- Glue stick
- Tape
- Ruler
- Googly eye
- An adult to help you

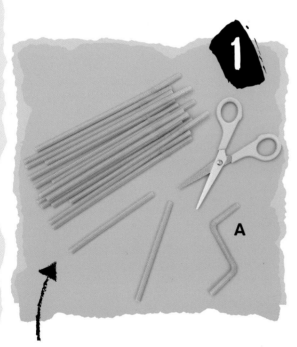

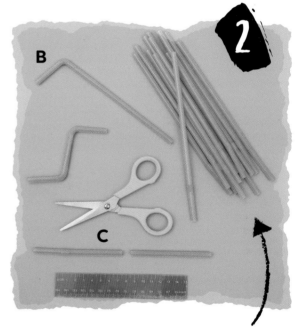

Ask an adult to help you cut the ends off two straws, leaving the same length of straw on either side of the bendy part. Insert one straw inside the other to form your flamingo's bent leg (A).

Bend the short part of a different straw to form the straight leg (B). Take another straw and cut it 2.5 inches (6 cm) above the bend (C). Bend this too, to form your flamingo's neck.

Cut a flamingo body and head shape from the pink paper. Use tape to attach the legs to the body and the neck to the head.

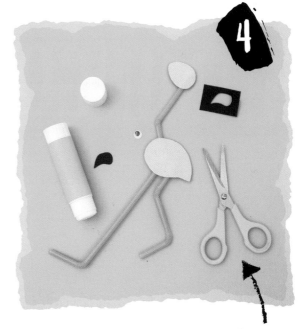

Stick the body parts together. Cut out a beak shape from black paper and glue it to the head. Glue on a googly eye.

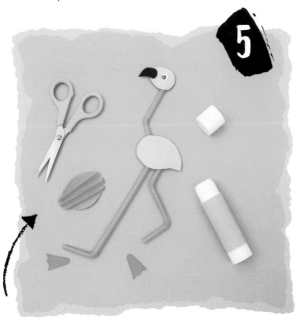

Cut out a circle of tissue paper and fold it like a fan. This will form the wing. Stick this to your flamingo, along with some feet made from orange paper.

DID YOU KNOW?

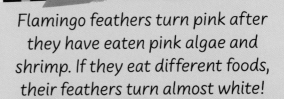

Flamingo feathers turn pink after they have eaten pink algae and shrimp. If they eat different foods, their feathers turn almost white!

FLAMINGO FACTS!

Huge flocks of lesser flamingos gather on Lake Bogoria in Kenya. They meet to feed on tiny algae, shrimp, and other creatures in the water.

They filter the food out of the water using their beak and tongue. When food starts to run out, they fly off to the next lake.

HIPPO FACTS!

Hippos only live in Africa. They spend most of the day keeping cool in water or mud. At night they graze on grass or fruit that has fallen to the ground.

Hippos are the second-largest land animal after the elephant. They are very heavy but can also run fast!

FLOATING HIPPO

Hippos spend a lot of time cooling off in water. Once you have made your hippo, try floating it in water!

YOU WILL NEED:

- Small water bottle
- Dark blue, white, black, and light blue foam
- Craft glue
- Scissors
- Masking tape
- An adult to help you

Screw the lid on the empty plastic water bottle. Wrap it in light blue foam and use glue to stick the foam down, where it overlaps. Use strips of masking tape to hold the foam in place until the glue dries.

Ask an adult to help you cut shapes from light blue foam. You need to cut out a B shape for the hippo's nose, a quarter of a circle (with the tip cut out), two ears, and a tail.

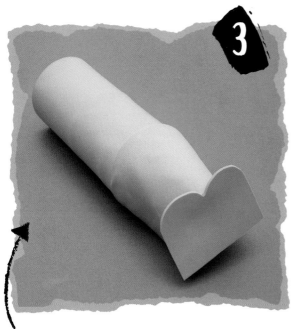

3

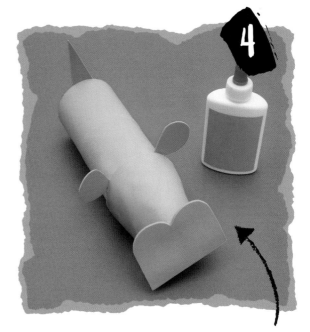

4

Glue the B-shaped nose onto the lid. Bend the quarter circle around the neck of the bottle and stick it in place to form the face.

Glue on the ears and tail. Leave to dry.

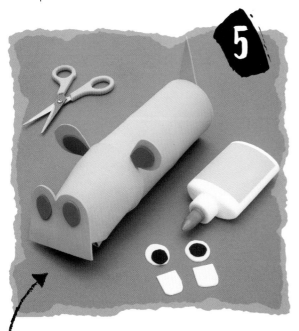

5

Cut out eyes from the black and white sheets of foam and glue them together. Now cut out teeth, inner ears, and nostrils as shown. Glue them in place.

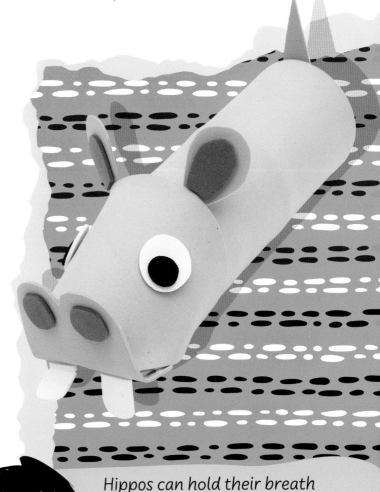

DID YOU KNOW?

Hippos can hold their breath underwater for five minutes! They can close their ears and nostrils to keep water out.

21

FOAM CHIMPANZEE

Wild chimpanzees live in forests, woodlands, and on the savanna. Their long arms help them swing through the trees to search for food or escape predators. Enjoy making your own foam chimpanzee!

1

Ask an adult to help with the cutting and stapling in this project. Cut four long strips of brown foam. Staple the ends of two of the strips to form rings, and staple these to the middle of the other strips.

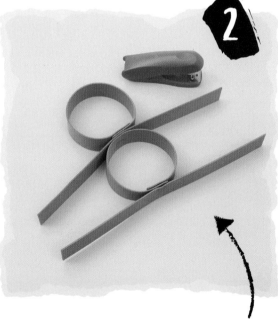

2

Staple the foam strips together so that the head and body rings form an 8 shape.

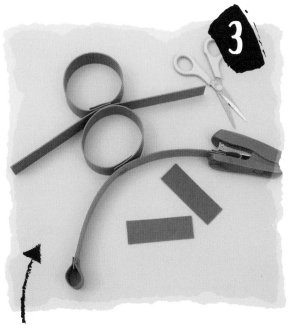

Cut four short strips of brown foam, bend them into a loop, and staple them to the ends of the long strips.

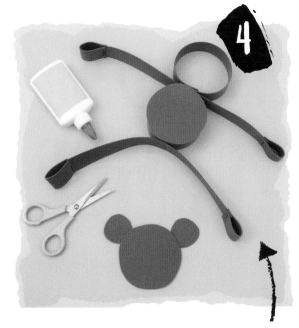

Cut two circles from brown foam to make a head and body for your chimpanzee. Cut out two small circles and glue them to the head.

Cut out a face, inner ears, and tummy from white foam. Now cut out eyes, a nose, a mouth, and a belly button from black foam. Glue them to your chimp.

DID YOU KNOW?

Chimpanzees are our nearest living relatives. Their hands are very much like ours, with thumbs that help them grip objects and use them as tools.

PRINTED PAPER LEMUR

Ring-tailed lemurs only live on the large island of Madagascar, off the coast of Africa. You can make your own ring-tailed lemur by doing some sponge printing!

YOU WILL NEED:

- White card stock
- Sponge
- Black and gray paint
- Black and yellow paper
- Glue stick
- Scissors
- Black felt-tip pen
- Paint palette
- An adult to help you

Put gray paint in the palette. Dip the sponge in the paint and press down lightly to create a patchy gray pattern to cover half the white card stock.

Clean the sponge and use it to paint black stripes on the other half of the card stock. Leave a section of the card stock white. Let the paint dry.

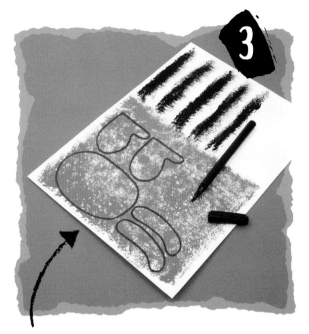

Ask an adult to help you draw the body, arms, and legs on the gray side of the card stock.

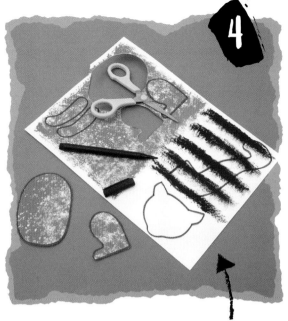

On the other side of the card stock, draw a curly tail on the striped part and a head on the white part. Cut out all the shapes.

Finish by cutting bits of gray card stock to form the top of the head and ear tufts, a black paper nose and eyes, and yellow circles. Glue all the pieces to the lemur. Add eye dots with the pen.

DID YOU KNOW?

Ring-tailed lemurs love to sunbathe! They can spend hours with their arms outstretched, soaking up the heat.

LEMUR FACTS!

The ring-tailed lemur is one of over 100 different kinds of lemurs that live in Madagascar.

The ring-tailed lemur's tail is longer than its body! It uses its tail as a flag when it walks through the forest so that others can see it.

MEERKAT FACTS!

A group of meerkats is called a mob. They work together to care for their young, dig burrows, gather food, and watch out for danger, such as snakes or eagles.

Meerkats belong to the mongoose family. Their babies are called pups.

A meerkat's long tail allows it to balance on its back legs so that it can stand upright.

LOOKOUT MEERKAT

Meerkats live in southern Africa in groups of up to 30 animals. They take turns acting as lookouts, standing on their back legs to watch out for danger.

YOU WILL NEED:

- Yogurt drink bottle
- Brown paper bag (or roll of brown paper)
- Card stock
- Glue stick
- Googly eyes
- Pencil
- Double-sided tape
- Tape
- Scissors
- Brown felt-tip pen
- An adult to help you

Stick strips of double-sided tape to the yogurt drink bottle. Cut a piece of brown paper from the bag or roll, peel off the back of the tape, and stick the paper to the bottle.

Cut a piece of brown paper the same size as the card stock and glue them together.

3

Fold the paper and card stock in half. Ask an adult to help you draw a meerkat head with the nose touching the fold. Cut it out.

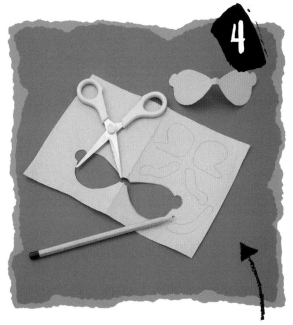

4

Now draw two arms, two legs, and a tail and cut them out.

5

Stick the arms, legs, and tail to the meerkat body. Glue googly eyes to the face and color the nose and ears with the brown felt-tip pen. Use tape to attach the head to the body.

DID YOU KNOW?

Meerkats have long claws for digging their underground burrows.

EGG CARTON
CAMEL

Camels live in the deserts of North Africa. This craft camel has a hump made from an egg carton!

1

Ask an adult to help you cut out one egg carton section. Cover it with yellow crepe paper, tucking any extra paper inside. Stick it in place.

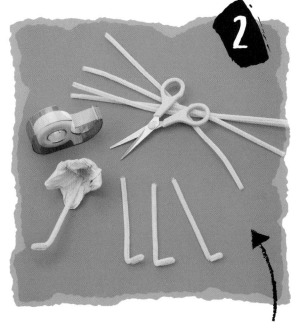

2

Cut two pipe cleaners in half so you have four pieces. Stick them with tape inside the egg carton section to form the camel's legs. Bend the ends to form feet.

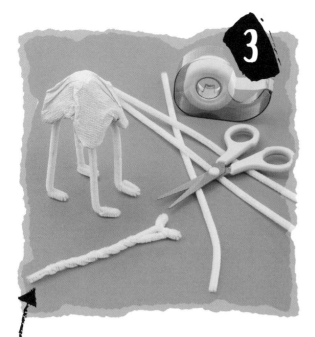

Twist two more pipe cleaners together to make the neck. Bend the ends over to make ears. Tape the other end under the body.

Make a tail out of a small section of pipe cleaner. Tape it to the back of the camel. Glue the pom-pom to the neck.

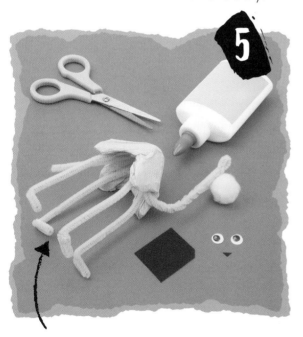

Glue googly eyes on the pom-pom. Cut out a small triangle of black card stock to make the nose and glue it to the pom-pom as well.

DID YOU KNOW?

North African people tamed camels thousands of years ago. They use them to carry goods and themselves across deserts.

GLOSSARY

algae tiny, plantlike living things

continent one of the very large areas of land on Earth, such as Africa, Europe, and Asia

grazing eating grasses and other plants

herd a group of animals

mane the long hair around a lion's face or on a horse's neck

migrate to move from one part of the world to another each year, often to find more food or better weather

predator an animal that eats other animals, or prey

savanna a flat area of land covered in grasses and a few trees

snorkel a tube held in the mouth at one end and sticking above the water's surface at the other

INDEX

Please visit our website, www.garethstevens.com. For a free color catalog of all our high-quality books, call toll free 1-800-542-2595 or fax 1-877-542-2596.

Published in 2025 by
Gareth Stevens Publishing
2544 Clinton St.
Buffalo, NY 14224

First published in Great Britain in 2022 by Wayland
Copyright © Hodder and Stoughton, 2022 Wayland
Acknowledgements:
Shutterstock: Volodymyr Burdiak 6; Andrey Gudkov 18, 26; JMx Images 19; Maggie Meyer 12; Walter Mario Stein 27; Tonyzhao 120 7; Kirill Trubitsyn 13.

Every effort has been made to clear copyright. Should there be any inadvertent omission please apply to the publisher for rectification.

Cataloging-in-Publication Data
Names: Lim, Annalees.
Title: African animal crafts / Annalees Lim.
Description: New York : Gareth Stevens Publishing, 2025. | Series: Animal arts and crafts | Includes glossary and index.
Identifiers: ISBN 9781538294352 (pbk.) | ISBN 9781538294369 (library bound) | ISBN 9781538294376 (ebook)
Subjects: LCSH: Handicraft--Juvenile literature. | Animals--Africa--Juvenile literature.
Classification: LCC TT160.L56 2025 | DDC 745.5--dc23

Editor, and author of the fact pages: Sarah Ridley
Design: Collaborate
Craft photography: Simon Pask, N1 Studios

CPSIA compliance information: Batch #CSGS25: For further information contact Gareth Stevens at 1-800-542-2595.

Find us on